This Peppa Pig book belongs to

ELLE BRADY

This book is based on the
TV Series 'Peppa Pig'
'Peppa Pig' is created by
Neville Astley and Mark Baker

Peppa Pig © Astley Baker Davies
Ltd/E1 Entertainment 2003

www.peppapig.com

Published by Ladybird Books Ltd 2010
A Penguin Company
Penguin Books Ltd, 80 Strand, London, WC2R 0RL, UK
Penguin Books Australia Ltd, Camberwell, Victoria, Australia
Penguin Books (NZ), 67 Appollo Drive, Rosedale, North Shore 0632,
New Zealand (a divison of Pearson New Zealand Ltd)

Contents

Follow the Rainbow!

Grunt! Grunt! Peppa and her family have spotted a rainbow.
Can you guess what is at the end of the rainbow?
Find your way through the maze to find out.

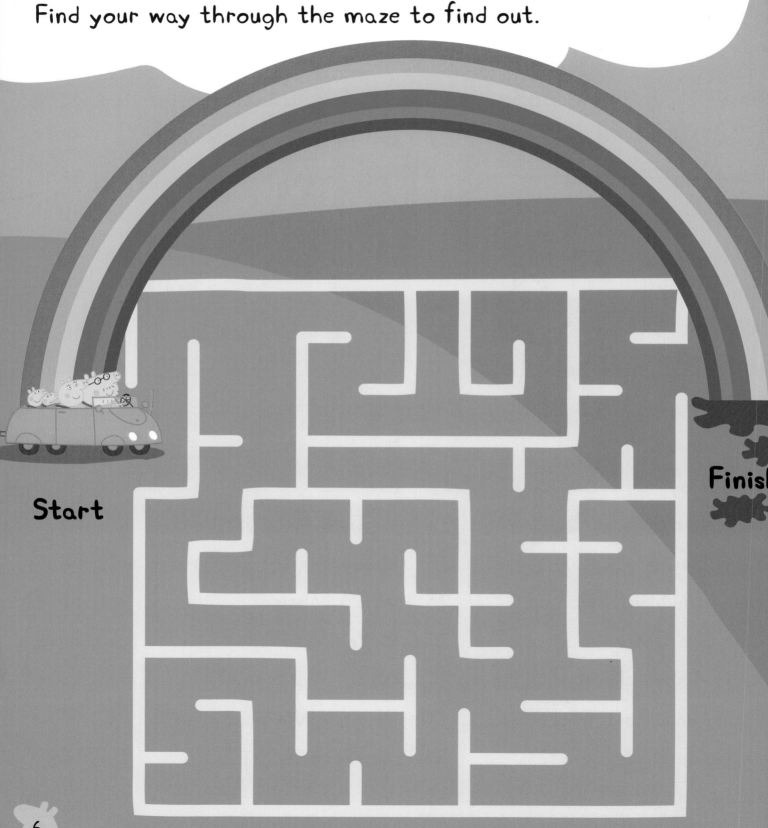

Start

Finish

6

Lovely Muddy Puddles

Peppa and George love jumping up and down in muddy puddles. Snort! Join the dots and colour the scene.

What's Your Favourite Toy?

Hooray! It's time for George and Peppa to play with their toys. George's favourite toy is his dinosaur. Grrrrr! Dine-saw! Peppa's favourite toy is her teddy bear. Draw your favourite toy in the space below.

Spot the Difference

George has Richard Rabbit over to play.
Snort! Can you spot the five differences
in the pictures below?

Yummy Favourite Flavours

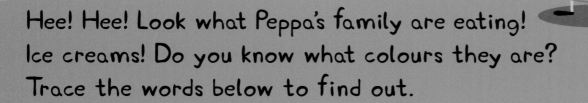

Hee! Hee! Look what Peppa's family are eating!
Ice creams! Do you know what colours they are?
Trace the words below to find out.

Daddy Pig's ice cream is **green.**

Mummy Pig's
ice cream is **orange.**

Peppa Pig's ice cream is **red.**

George's ice cream is **blue.**

10

Who's Next?

Find the right stickers to put on the white shapes.
Snort! Snort!

Answers: 1. Princess Peppa. 2. Sir George the Brave. 3. Daddy Pig. 4. Emily Elephant.

11

All Work and No Play

One sunny morning, Daddy Pig was reading his newspaper in the garden.
Just then, Mummy Pig came outside holding Daddy Pig's briefcase.
"Daddy Pig! You'll be late for work!" says Mummy Pig.
"But it's Saturday, Mummy Pig! Isn't it?" Daddy Pig asks.

"No, it's Thursday," replies Mummy Pig.
"Arrrgghhh!" shouts Daddy Pig
and jumps into his car.
Poor Daddy Pig has to go to
work after all.

Mummy Pig is going to work today,
so it's time for George and
Peppa to go to playgroup.
Mummy Sheep and Suzy
Sheep come to pick them up.
Baaa! Hello, Peppa!" says Suzy Sheep.
"Grunt! Hello, Suzy!" cries Peppa.
Everyone waves goodbye and
Mummy Pig drives off.

At playgroup, Madame Gazelle tells the
children it is time to play shops.
"Peppa and Suzy can be shopkeepers. Everyone else
can be customers," instructs Madame Gazelle.
Peppa and Suzy are very pleased.
"I will take the money, Suzy, and you can stack
the shelves. Snort!" Peppa says.

Danny Dog is the first customer at the shop.
"Woof! Hello, shopkeeper, can I have some
biscuits, please?" Danny Dog asks politely.
Suzy looks on the shelves but can't find any biscuits.
She finds a toy telephone instead.
"That will be a hundred pounds, please," says Peppa.
"Kerch-ching!" goes the cash register.

Pedro Pony is the second customer at the shop.
"Neigh! Can I have a loaf of bread, please?" he asks.
Suzy looks on the shelves but can't find a toy loaf of bread.
She finds a toy house instead.
Oh dear. Pedro Pony doesn't have any money.
"You can pay us next time you come in,"
Peppa says, kindly.

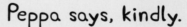

"Hee! Hee! Ha! Ha! Woof! Grunt!"
cry all the children at the end of
playgroup. Daddy Pig comes to
pick up Peppa and George.
"Daddy, have you had a busy day?"
Peppa asks.
"Yes, I've been working very hard,"
Daddy replies.
"We've been working very hard,
too!" says Suzy Sheep.

When they reach home, they run inside to find Mummy Pig
and George on the computer playing Happy Mrs Chicken.
"Naughty Mummy! You're playing Happy Mrs Chicken!" exclaims Peppa.
"That's because George and I have finished our work.
Haven't we, George?" says Mummy Pig.
"We've all finished our work, so let's all play!" cries Daddy Pig.

Where is Princess Peppa?

There are lots of Princess Peppas hiding in this picture. Every time you see a Peppa, point to her and shout, "Oink!"

What else can you see?

Rhyme Time

Read this lovely Peppa rhyme. When you see a picture say the word out loud.

 and  are ready to go,

To spend a day out in the ,

 and  are coming too,

To make a  - there's so much to do!

Back inside, when it's time for bed,

 and  are sleepyheads!

 Peppa

 George

 Snow

 Mummy Pig

 Daddy Pig

 Snowman

18

Matching

Peppa and her friends love their toys.
Can you find the stickers to
match the toys?

Colour by Numbers

Hooray! It's time to play shop at playgroup.
Use the blobs of colour to help you finish the
picture of Peppa playing shop with her friends.

How Many Blocks?

Can you count how many blocks George an Peppa are playing with?

There are _____ square blocks.

There are _____ triangle blocks.

What other shapes can you see?

Piggy Playtime

Brrrr! It's cold outside and Peppa's family are playing outside in their woolly clothes. Use your colours to finish the picture.

Muddy Puddles!

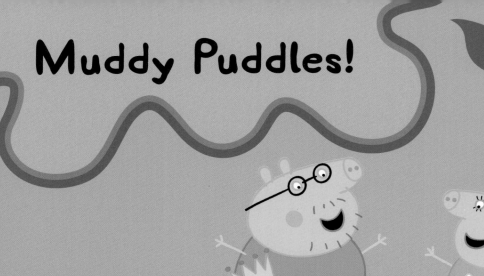

Hooray! It's been raining outside. What do Peppa, her family and friends like to do when it rains? Jump in muddy puddles! Trace the words to complete the story.

Peppa and George jump in muddy **puddles.**

Mummy and Daddy jump in muddy **puddles.**

Snort! Snort! Everyone is having **fun.**

Odd One Out

Peppa and her family are going for a camper van ride.
There is something in the camper van that shouldn't be there.
Can you circle what it is?

Richard Rabbit Comes to Play

Peppa and George are in the playroom stacking blocks on top of one another. Today, George is very happy. Snort! He has his friend Richard Rabbit coming over to play. Ding, dong!
"George! Richard Rabbit is here!"
Daddy Pig shouts from downstairs.

George and Richard play with a ball. Boing
The ball bounces and knocks Peppa's blocks.
"Please play something less bouncy!"
cries Peppa.

"Dine-saw! Grrr!" growls George.
George and Richard turn the playroom into Dinosaur Land!
"Roar! Roar! Grrr!" George and Richard shout.
Peppa is not happy.
"I'm leaving! Grunt! It's too noisy!" Peppa says.

Peppa invites her friend, Suzy Sheep to play. Dinosaur Land is now
a hospital. "I'm the Doctor. Hmm. This dinosaur looks sick," grunts
Peppa. "And this dinosaur is a very purpley ill colour."
Richard and George now don't have their dinosaurs. They don't want
their dinosaurs in bed. They are not happy.

George puts on a train driver's hat and Richard Rabbit
blows a whistle. The bedroom is now a railway station.
Choo! Choo!

Oh dear. Peppa and Suzy Sheep are not happy.
Peppa stomps over to her toys and puts on her wings and crown.
"There aren't any trains in Fairy Land!" shouts Peppa.
"Whaaa!" cry George and Richard Rabbit.

"Grunt! What's all this crying about?" asks Mummy Pig.
"George and Richard want to play dinosaurs and trains," says Peppa.
"And we want to play hospitals and fairies," says Suzy Sheep.

"Maybe you could all play outside?" suggests Daddy Pig. "After it's been raining in the garden, what do you normally find?"
Muddy puddles of course! Everyone rushes outside and jumps up and down in the muddy puddles. Baa! Squeak! Grunt! Hooray!

Going on a Boat Trip

Oink! Oink! Grandpa Pig is taking Peppa and George on a boat ride. Circle what they are going to take with them.

Happy or Sad?

How do Peppa and George feel today?
Are they smiling, frowning or pulling a funny face?
Use your pencils to finish drawing their faces.

Counting Fun

Grunt! Grunt!
Everyone loves jumping in muddy puddles!
Count how many people are jumping and
write the number in the box below.

Page 11

Page 19

Page 56-57

Page 42-43

Page 45

Best Friends

Suzy is a

sheep.

Richard is a

rabbit.

Candy is a

cat.

George and Peppa are

pigs.

Cut and Paste

Peppa and her family are in their living room. Complete the scene by cutting out coloured shapes to fit the white spaces.

Ask an adult to help you with this activity.

You will need:

Scissors
Glue
Old magazines or coloured paper

Polly's Boat Trip

Today, Grandpa Pig is taking Peppa and George on a boat trip. Polly Parrot is going, too.
"Grandpa Pig! Have you got your mobile telephone?" Granny Pig asks.
"Yes, Granny Pig!" replies Grandpa Pig. Grandpa Pig starts the engine and the boat begins to sail away. Peppa, Grandpa Pig and Polly Parrot all wave goodbye to Granny Pig.

Sailing down the river, Grandpa Pig sees his best friend, Granddad Dog, cleaning his boat. "Ho! Ho! I don't know why you bother cleaning that rusty boat! I'm surprised it's still afloat!" jokes Grandpa Pig.
"This rusty boat will still be afloat long after your old tin boat has sunk to the bottom of the river!" laughs Granddad Dog, playfully.

Grandpa Pig, Peppa, George and Polly sail on down the river. "Now, I am the captain of this boat and when the captain tells you to do something, you must do it," explains Grandpa Pig.

"Aye! Aye! Captain!" shout Peppa and George.
Peppa wants to be the captain, so Grandpa Pig gives her his captain's hat. Peppa loves being the captain.
Captain Peppa is a bit bossy.

"Perhaps I should be the captain again? We don't want to crash into anything! Snort!" says Grandpa Pig.
Crash! The boat runs aground into a sand bank.
"Don't worry! I'll ring Granny Pig. She can get help!" says Grandpa Pig.

Polly the Parrot squawks in Grandpa Pig's ear and gives him a fright. "Beep! Beep! Boop! Boop!" she says. Oh dear. Grandpa Pig drops the phone overboard. What are they going to do?

"Snort! I know! Polly can fly to Granny!" says Peppa. Grandpa Pig teaches Polly what to say to Granny.

Granny Pig is a home and Polly Parrot lands on the telephone "Oh! Hello, Polly What are you doing here? Granny Pig asks "Squawk! Grandpa Pig say Snort! Help! Help!" says Poll

"Goodness me, Grandpa must need help!" says Granny Pig

Granny Pig and Polly Parrot jump in the car and drive to the river. They see Granddad Dog on his boat. "Grandpa Pig needs help! Please could you rescue him? Granny Pig asks. "Madame, I would be delighted! Woof!" barks Granddad Dog.

Granddad Dog sails his boat to rescue
Grandpa Pig, Peppa and George.
"Would you like my rusty old boat to rescue you?"
asks Granddad Dog.
"Aye! Aye! Skipper! Snort!" says Grandpa Pig.
Everyone is happy. They all think Polly is a very clever parrot.
"I'm a clever parrot!" says Polly and everyone laughs.

Copy Colouring

George is hiding from Peppa under the table. Use the small picture to help you colour the picture below.

Dot-to-Dot

Grunt! Snort! Peppa is riding her bicycle. Join the dots, then colour in the picture.

Ship Ahoy!

Aye! Aye! Captain!
Grandpa Pig is captain of the ship. Can you find some stickers to finish this picture?

Who Said That?

Draw a line to the noise each animal makes.

Grunt!

Baaa!

Woof!

Meow!

Spot the Difference

Peppa and George have gone to visit Grandpa Pig in the garden. Can you find the five differences between the pictures?

Add a flower sticker to the page, as you find each one.

Answers: 1. The shovel has disappeared. 2. Grandpa Pig is wearing a different hat. 3. A cloud has appeared. 4. Grandpa Pig's clothes have changed colour. 5. A lettuce has moved.

Favourite Foods

Yum! It's dinner time for Peppa's family. What is your favourite food? Draw it in the space below.

What Can You See?

Look who is in the garden! Can you fill in the boxes below?

There are _____ apples in the garden.

Grandpa Pig and _____ Pig are wearing hats.

There are _____ trees in the garden.

There is a _____ for apples.

Peppa Ears

Make your own Peppa ears using the instructions below.

Ask an adult to help you with this activity.

Stick on headband

Stick on headband

What to do:

1. When you have finished reading this book, ask an adult to cut out the ears and headband strips.
2. Glue or tape the pig ears to the headband.
3. Ask an adult to fit the band around your head and stick the ends together with tape.
4. Oink like Peppa! Snort! Snort!

Hee hee ha hoo. Grunt! Grunt! Hee Hee Ha. Ho ho ho ha. Ha ha ha. Grunt!

Hee hee ha hoo. Grunt! Grunt! Hee Hee Ha. Ho ho ho ha. Ha ha ha. Grunt!

Hee hee ha hoo. Grunt! Grunt! Hee Hee Ha. Ho ho ho ha. Ha ha ha. Grunt!

It's Time to Play! Hooray!

Peppa loves playing shopkeeper at playgroup. Answer the questions by pointing to the right place in the picture.

Where is the
toy train?

Where is
Rebecca Rabbit?

Who is the first
customer at
Peppa's shop?

Where is
the clock?

Who is holding
the telephone?

What is your
favourite toy in
the picture?

Colours in the Rainbow

Peppa has spotted a rainbow. Use the number key to colour in the picture.

1
2
3
4
5
6
7
4
4
4
2

KEY

1 2 3

4 5 6 7

What's Missing?

Oh dear! It's raining and Daddy Pig is getting wet!
What does he need to stay dry?
Use your pencils to finish the picture.

I'm Princess Peppa!

Grunt! Snort! Colour in this picture of Princess Peppa.

What's Your Name?

Peppa has written her name on the board.
Can you write your name too?

Peppa

My name is

....

Wriggly Worms!

Snort! Snort! Peppa and George have found some rather wriggly worms. Decorate the picture with your stickers and colour it in.

The Rainbow

Today, Peppa and her family are going for a drive in the mountains.
"Snort! Are we there yet?" asks Peppa.
"Hee! Hee! Not yet, Peppa," says Mummy Pig.
Peppa and George sigh. Car trips can sometimes be a bit boring.

"Grunt! I know a game we can play! We each have to spot a car with our favourite colour," says Daddy Pig.
Look! Candy Cat and her family are driving in their car.
"Ho! Ho! Green! That's my favourite colour. I win!" Daddy Pig says.

Look! Danny Dog is driving in Granddad Dog's orange truck.
"Orange! So I win!" says Mummy Pig.
"This is a silly game! Grunt! There isn't a red car anywhere!" says Peppa Pig.
"There is one red car on the road," says Daddy Pig.
"What colour is our car?"
"It's red!" says Peppa.
"My favourite colour! I win! I win! Hee! Hee! Hee!"

The car climbs up and up the mountain until it reaches the top.
Everyone gets out of the car.
"Look at the lovely sunny view," says Daddy Pig.
It starts to pour with rain and everyone starts to get very wet.
"Arrrrgh!" they all cry.

Daddy Pig spots Miss Rabbit's ice cream stall.
"Hello, Miss Rabbit. Four ice creams, please," says Daddy Pig.
"What flavours would you like?" asks Miss Rabbit.
"Mint, orange, strawberry and blueberry, please," says Daddy Pig.

Everyone is very happy. They all have ice cream in their favourite colour
They sit in the car, eat their yummy ice cream and watch the rain.
"Mmmm, yummy! Hee! Hee! Grunt!" everyone says.

"Look! The sun has come out!" says Mummy Pig.
"A rainbow! Hee! Hee!" giggles Peppa.
Peppa and George love rainbows.
"Look! It has all our favourite colours in it," says Mummy Pig.

What's at the end of the rainbow?
The family chase the rainbow in the car to find out.
"Daddy! Have you found the rainbow's treasure?" asks Peppa.
"Grunt! Yes! I have!" says Daddy Pig.
A big muddy puddle! They all jump in the puddle together.
"This is the best rainbow treasure ever!" says Peppa.

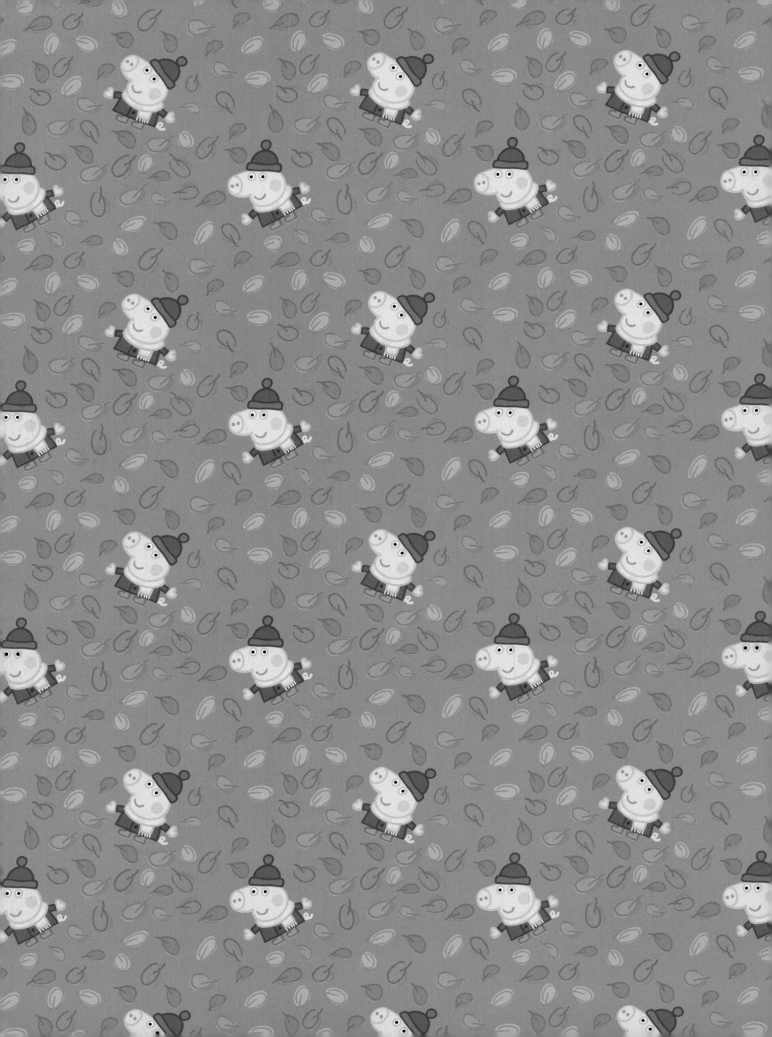